I0117505

C. A. Mecaskey & Co.

Songs Adrift

Gems from an old scrap book

C. A. Mecaskey & Co.

Songs Adrift
Gems from an old scrap book

ISBN/EAN: 9783337265540

Printed in Europe, USA, Canada, Australia, Japan

Cover: Foto ©Thomas Meinert / pixelio.de

More available books at **www.hansebooks.com**

SONGS ADRIFT.

GE[...]M AN OLD SCRAP BOOK.

[SI]XTH EDITION.

[...]S."

[PHIL]ADELPHIA:

[...]CASKEY & CO.

[8]08 CHESTNUT STREET.

1874.

ANNOUNCEMENT.

In presenting a new edition of SONGS ADRIFT to our friends, we are guided entirely by the sentiments of those who have read the earlier issues. Our little book has been received with unexpected favor, and we trust it will continue to please. A number of changes have been made in the matter, and as an additional attraction we have inserted an original frontispiece, drawn expressly for us by Mr. A. F. Bunner.

"SONGS ADRIFT."

——oo¡o¡oo——

It is surprising how many really good and stirring poems go float-
ing up and down the currents of the great sea of literature, with never
an author to claim them, and never a publisher to gather them into a
volume. They take their start in a corner of a weekly paper, or deep
in the recesses of a magazine, are scissored from one paper to another,
and at last find quiet resting places in somebody's scrap-book. They
are usually the one or two heart-stirring songs of a poet who is never
able to match them afterwards, and who, in despair, abandons them to
their fate; but sometimes they are the isolated ones which the world se-
lects to remember, while the volume containing their duller companions
slumbers unread on a forgotten shelf; and sometimes they are the only
songs which some master-mind of prose has permitted itself to sing;
but in any case they have no home, no associations, no harbor of
refuge—literary waifs on a sea which has shipwrecked their companions
by thousands, they belong to the finder; and even the king can scarcely
hope to apply to them the law of FLOTSAM AND JETSAM.

Mainly of this sort are the scraps collected in this little volume. A few of them are by well-known authors, a few more by rising ones, but the majority are to be credited to that convenient authority, "Mr. Anonymous." So far as we know, none of them—or but one or two, at most—are contained in a published edition of their author's works; and as we could name the writers of so few, we have deemed it best to withhold the author's name, even where it was known.

The Poems are from a scrap-book, and are given here as they stood there, without order or arrangement, but just as the periodical currents drifted them in. Like the emotions they express, they will be found to relate to almost every phase of life and life's experience. SOMEBODY will be grateful for each one of them; and to that somebody the one he or she likes best—and to all our friends the volume in general—is respectfully dedicated by

Their Obedient Servants,

C. A. M. & Co.

THE OLD CANOE.

HERE the rocks are gray and the shore is steep,
And the waters below look dark and deep,
Where the rugged pine in its gloomy pride
Leans gloomily over the murky tide,
Where the reeds and the rushes are tall and
    rank,
And the weeds grow thick on the winding
    bank,
Where the shadow is heavy the whole day
    through,
Lies at its moorings the old canoe.

The useless paddles are idly dropped,
Like a sea bird's wings that the storm hath lopped,
And crossed on the railing one o'er one,
Like folded hands when the work is done;
While busily back and forth between
The spider stretches his silvery screen,
And the solemn owl, with his dull "too-hoo,"
Nestles down on the side of the old canoe.

The stern half sunk in the slimy wave,
Rots slowly away in its living grave,
And the green moss creeps o'er its dull decay,
Hiding the mouldering dust away,
Like the hand that plants o'er the tomb a flower,
Or the ivy that mantles a fallen tower;
While many a blossom of liveliest hue
Springs up o'er the stern of the old canoe.

The currentless waters are dead and still;
But the light winds play with the boat at will,
And lazily in and out again,
It floats the length of its rusty chain,
Like the weary march of the hands of time,
That meet and part at the noontide chime;
And the shore is kissed at each turn anew
By the dripping bow of the old canoe.

Oh, many a time with a careless hand
I have pushed away from the pebbly strand,
And paddled down where the stream ran quick—
Where the whirls were wild and the foam ran thick;
And laughed as I leaned o'er the rocking side,
And looked below in the broken tide,
To see that the faces and boats were two,
That were mirrored back from the old canoe.

But now, as I lean o'er the crumbling side,
And look below in the sluggish tide,
The face that I see is graver grown,
And the laugh that I hear has a sober tone,
And the hands that lent to the light skiff wings
Have grown familiar with sterner things;
But I love to think of the hours that flew
As I rocked where the whirls their wild spray threw,
Ere the blossoms waved or the green grass grew
O'er the mouldering stern of the old canoe.

On the Banks of the Beautiful River.

LIKE a foundling in slumber the summer-day lay,
    On the crimsoning threshold of Even,
And I thought that the glow from the "azure-arched"
      way,
    Was a glimpse of the coming of heaven.
There together we sat by the beautiful stream;
We had nothing to do but to love and to dream
    In the days that have gone on before.
These are not the same days, though they bear the
      same name
With the ones I shall welcome no more!

But it may be the angels are calling them o'er,
    For a Sabbath and summer forever,
When the years shall forget the Decembers they wore,
    And the shroud shall be woven, no, never!
In a twilight like that, Jenny June for a bride,
Oh, what more of the world could one wish for beside?
    As we gazed on the river enrolled,
Till we heard, or we fancied, its musical tide,
    As it flowed through the gate-way of gold.

"Jenny June," then I said, "let us linger no more
    On the banks of the beautiful river;
Let the boat be unmoored, and be muffled the oar,
    And we'll steal into Heaven together.
If the angel on duty our coming descries,
You have nothing to do but throw off the disguise
    That you wore when you wandered with me,
And the sentry shall say, 'Welcome back to the skies,
    We have long been a-waiting for thee.'"

Oh, how sweetly she spoke ere she uttered a word,
    With that blush partly her's, partly Even's;
And that tone like the dream of a song we once heard,
    As she whispered, "that way is not Heaven's;
For the river that runs by the realms of the blest
Has no song in its ripple, no star on its breast—
    Oh, that river is nothing like this!
For it glides on in shadow, beyond the world's west,
    Till it breaks into beauty and bliss!"

I am lingering yet, but I linger alone,
    On the banks of the beautiful river;
'Tis the TWIN of that day, but the wave where it shone,
    Bears the willow-tree's shadow forever!

BOB WHITE.

ALF way ripe is the wavy wheat,
   Abroad in the fields where it stands breast
      high;
Soft as a whisper, and strangely sweet,
   The breath of the wind as it wanders by;
         "Bob White!"
Hark! whose is it, the voice I hear?
Calling aloud in the tall grain near—
         "Bob White!"

Hotter each day grows the warm June sun,
   A shade more purple the sky's deep blue,
And the bright June roses have just begun
   To sprinkle their leaves with an ashen hue;
         "Bob White!"
There it is calling, again and again,
Sweet and clear from the amber grain—
         "Bob White!"

" What does the little bird say, my son?"
       The father asks of his fair haired boy,
Where over the porch the wild vines run,
       And the humming bee murmurs his song of joy.
                              " Bob White!"
Sounding aloud as the voice draws nigh,
And the innocent lips of the child reply—
                              "Bob White!"

One shrill note and a whirr of wings
       Away in a moment, flying low,
As over the loose wall lightly spring
       The farmer lad with his rake and hoe;
                              "Bob White!"
Whistles the boy, while his big black eyes
Follow the flock wherever it flies—
                              "Bob White!"

A soft, sleek coat of a darkish brown,
       And a speckled waistcoat of lighter shade,
Passing to white where it reaches down,
       With breeches of chestnut trimly made;
                              " Bob White!"
This is he whom we hear repeat,
All day long in the ripening wheat—
    ·   "Bob White!"

Two half circles around the throat,
   One pale streak on his lordship's crown,
And all over the back of his Quaker coat
   Paler streaks of a yellowish brown ;
               "Bob White!"
This is he who fattens and thrives,
Down in the wheat where he calls to his wives—
               "Bob White!"

A famous Mormon is he, I'm told,
   Full of love for the softer sex ;
With a heart like an eagle's, quick and bold,
   And a spirit fiery and easy to vex ;
               "Bob White!"
Is it his own or another's name
That he keeps repeating always the same—
               "Bob White!"

A few dried leaves and some tufts of hay
   Under a tuft of sheltering grass ;
Hid in a hollow out of the way,
   Where only by chance a foot may pass—
               "Bob White!"
Thus he calls now, the nest is made—
Thus he will call till the eggs are laid !
               "Bob White!"

Yellowish white the brittle shell,
    Speckled with brown like his own little breast,
Watched, and tended, and guarded well,
    A dozen or more in the homely nest ;
                            " Bob White ! "
Far less frequent, and somewhat dry
The voice of our friend, as the days go by,
                            " Bob White ! "

A smart young fellow, his son and heir,
    Ready at once from the nest to roam ;
Little of trouble and little of care
    Brings the boy to the mother at home ;
                            "Bob White ! "
Almost silenced the once clear tone,
Now that the season of love is flown,
                            " Bob White ! "

There in the grass where the dew hangs damp,
    Ever watchful of any harm ;
Back to back in a circular camp,
    Ready to rise at the least alarm ;
                            "Bob White ! "
Sits from the time the twilight falls,
All through the night, while no shrill throat calls
                            " Bob White ! "

By-and-by when the summer is dead,
   And the glowing hand of autumn weaves
Gorgeous patterns of purple and red,
    With gold and brown in the orchard's leaves;—
           "Bob White!"
Down in the stubble piping low,
No longer shall call as the bright days go—
           "Bob White!"

THE GIRL FOR ME.

UST fair enough to be pretty,
　　Just gentle enough to be sweet,
Just saucy enough to be witty,
　　Just dainty enough to be neat.

Just tall enough to be graceful,
　　Just slight enough for a fay,
Just dress enough to be tasteful,
　　Just merry enough to be gay.

Just tears enough to be tender,
　　Just sighs enough to be sad,
Tones soft enough to remember,
　　Your heart through the cadence made glad.

Just meek enough for submission,
　　Just bold enough to be brave,
Just pride enough for ambition,
　　Just thoughtful enough to be grave.

A tongue that can talk without harming,
    Just mischief enough to tease,
Manners pleasant enough to be charming,
    That put you at once at your ease.

Disdain for to put presumption,
    Sarcasm to answer a fool,
Cool contempt shown to assumption,
    Proper dignity always the rule.

Flights of fairy fancy ethereal,
    Devotion to science full paid,
Stuff of the sort of material,
    Poets and painters are made.

Generous enough, and kind-hearted,
    Pure as the angels above;
O, from her may I never be parted,
    For such is the maiden I love.

TRUE WORTH.

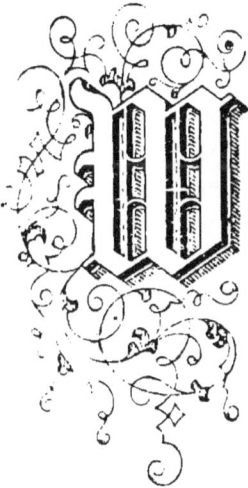

WHO shall judge a man from manners?
    Who shall know him by his dress?
Paupers may be fit for princes,
    Princes fit for something less.
Crumpled shirt and dirty jacket
    May beclothe the golden ore
Of the humblest thoughts and feelings—
    Satin vests would do no more.

There are springs of crystal nectar,
    Ever welling out of stone;
There are purple buds and golden,
    Hidden, crushed and overthrown;
God, who counts by souls, not dresses,
    Loves and prospers you and me,
While he values thrones the highest,
    But as pebbles in the sea.

SONGS ADRIFT

Man, upraised above his fellows,
　　Oft forgets his fellows then;
Masters, rulers, lords, remember—
　　That your meanest hands are men—
Men by labor, men by feeling,
　　Men by thought, and men by fame,
Claiming equal rights to sunshine,
　　In man's ennobling name.

There are foam-embroidered oceans,
　　There are little reed-clad rills;
There are feeble, inch-high saplings,
　　There are cedars on the hills:
God, who counts by souls, not stations,
　　Loves and prospers you and me;
For to him all vain distinctions
　　Are as pebbles in the sea.

Toiling hands alone are builders
　　Of a nation's wealth or fame;
Titled laziness is pensioned,
　　Fed and fattened on the same;
By the sweat of others' foreheads,
　　Living only to rejoice,
While the poor man's outraged freedom
　　Vainly lifteth up its voice.

SONGS ADRIFT

Truth and justice are eternal,
    Born with loveliness and light,
Secret wrongs shall never prosper
    While there is a sunny right;
God, whose world-heard voice is singing
    Boundless love to you and me,
Sinks oppression with its titles,
    As the pebbles of the sea.

COMING HOME.

BROTHERS and sisters growing old,
    Do you all remember yet,
That home in the shade of the rustling trees,
    Where once the household met?

Do you know how we used to come from school,
    Through summer's pleasant heat;
With the yellow fennel's golden dust
    On our tired little feet?

And sometimes in an idle mood,
    We loitered by the way;
And stopped in the woods to gather flowers,
    And in the fields to play?

Till warned by the deep'ning shadows fall,
    That told of the coming night,
We climbed on the top of the last long hill,
    And saw our home in sight?

And brothers and sisters, older now,
  Than she whose life is o'er,
Do you think of the mother's loving face,
  That looked from the open door?

Alas, for the changing things of time;
  That form in the dust is low;
And that loving home was hid from us,
  In the darkness, long ago!

And we have come to life's last hill,
  From which our weary eyes,
Can almost look on that home that shines,
  Eternal in the skies.

For that mother, who waited for us here,
  Wearing a smile so sweet,
Now waits on the hills of Paradise,
  For her children's coming feet!

PLAYING AT COURTING.

LET'S play at courting, little wife—
    Forget these boys and girls,
Ignore the wrinkles on our brows,
    The gray hair 'mid our curls.

"Me, John, across the field you see,
    With Sunday-suit bedight;
You at the glass push back your hair,
    And smooth your apron white.

"You hum above your work, while loud
    And quick your heart beats on ;
And yet unconscious look, as if
    There never was a John.

"Well, I am there: I dare not kiss
    The little hand I touch;
It seems, just sitting by your side,
    Almost one joy too much.

" And, as your shining needles move,
　　'Tis bliss enough to see
The downcast lashes sometimes lift,
　　To steal a glance at me.

" The neighbors shy look in sometimes—
　　I do not call them here;
I'd rather not, to tell the truth,
　　Have anybody near.

" The old folks bid a pleased good-night,
　　And leave us two together—
To think, and blush, and nothing say,
　　Except, ''Tis pleasant weather.'

" But some way, by-and-by (how is't?
　　I never could define,)
My hand gets snuggling round your waist,
　　And yours gets clasped in mine.

" And some way, stranger still, your cheek
　　Comes very near my own;
For thus I bend my head, to hear
　　That bashful, whispering tone—

" And then "—wife nudged me—Close behind,
　　Eyes opened wide to see,
Our eldest stood—she's just the age
　　Her mother married me.

IF I SHOULD DIE TO-NIGHT

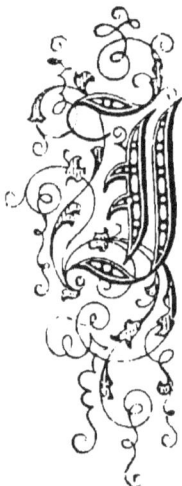

F I should die to-night,
My friends would look upon my quiet face
Before they laid it in its resting place,
And deem that death had left it almost fair;
And, laying snow-white flowers against my hair
Would smooth it down with tearful tenderness,
And fold my hands with lingering caress.
    Poor hands, so empty and so cold to-night

If I should die to-night,
My friends would call to-mind, with loving thought,
Some kindly deed the icy hand had wrought;
Some gentle word the frozen lips had said;
Errands on which the willing feet had sped—
The memory of my selfishness and pride,
My hasty words, would all be put aside,
    And so I should be loved and mourned to-night.

If I should die to-night,
Even hearts estranged would turn once more to me,
Recalling other days remorsefully.
The eyes that chill me with averted glance
Would look upon me as of yore, perchance,
And soften in the old, familiar way,
For who could war with dumb, unconscious clay?
So I might rest, forgiven of all, to-night.

Oh! friends, I pray to-night,
Keep not your kisses for my dead, cold brow.
The way is lonely; let me feel them now.
Think gently of me; I am travel worn.
My faltering feet are pierced with many a thorn.
Forgive, Oh! hearts estranged, forgive, I plead!
When dreamless rest is mine I shall not need
The tenderness for which I long to-night.

SEPTEMBER.

WEET is the voice that calls
  From babbling water-falls,
In meadows where the downy seeds are flying;
  And soft the breezes blow,
  And eddying come and go,
In faded gardens where the rose is dying.

  Among the stubbled corn
  The blithe quail pipes at morn,
The merry partridge drums in hidden places,
  And glittering insects gleam
  Above the reedy stream
Where busy spiders spin their filmy laces.

  At eve cool shadows fall
  Across the garden wall,
And on the clustered grapes to purple turning;
  And pearly vapors lie
  Along the eastern sky
Where the broad harvest-moon is redly burning.

SONGS ADRIFT

Ah, soon on field and hill
The winds shall whistle chill,
And patriarch swallows call their flocks together
To fly from frost and snow
And seek for lands where blow
The fairer blossoms of a balmier weather.

The pollen-dusted bees
Search for the honey-lees
That linger in the last flowers of September;
While plaintive mourning doves
Coo sadly to their loves
Of the dead summer they so well remember.

The cricket chirps all day,
"O, fairest summer, stay!"
The squirrel eyes askance the chestnuts browning;
The wild-fowl fly afar
Above the foamy bar,
And hasten southward ere the skies are frowning.

Now comes a fragrant breeze
Through the dark cedar trees,
And round about my temples fondly lingers
In gentle playfulness,
Like to the soft caress
Bestowed in happier days by loving fingers.

Yet, though a sense of grief
Comes with the falling leaf,
And memory makes the summer doubly pleasant,
    In all my autumn dreams,
    A future summer gleams,
Passing the fairest glories of the present!

F A I T H.

CHEER up, dear heart! I know the way is weary,
    And the stones rough unto thy tender feet;
I know the walk is sad and dark and dreary,
    And seems so far until our pathways meet.
Cheer up, dear love! Time's hand upon the dial,
    I know, so slowly marks the creeping hours,
That thy heart faints beneath the wearying
        trial,
    As roses die awaiting summer showers.

Cheer up, my own! I know thy life is lonely;
    Lone as a night, with neither moon nor star:
And O, if I could cheer and soothe it only,
    By words that come thus to thee from afar!
If I can know, thy woman's faith, endering,
    Still lives beneath the darkness of that sky,
Still dreams of joys, the heart to hope alluring,
    That e'en grow dearer as they seem to die.

5*

Cheer up, dear Love! I know thy tears are falling,
  Would I were near to kiss them from thy cheek !
I know thy heart is faint, and fainter growing;
  Though not thy faith, and not thy love more weak.
Cheer up, dear one! the ocean waves are beating,—
  In vain against the rock far out at sea;
So let thy heart in proud resistance meeting,
  Conquer the fate that keeps me far from thee.

Had you ever a Cousin, Tom?

AD you ever a cousin, Tom?
    Did your cousin happen to sing?
Sisters we've all by the dozen, Tom,
    But a cousin's a different thing.
There's something in a sister's lip,
    When you give her a good-night kiss,
That savors so much of relationship,
    That nothing occurs amiss.
But a cousin's lip, if you once unite
    With yours in the quietest way,
Instead of sleeping a wink that night,
    You'll be dreaming the following day.

No one thinks any harm, Tom,
    With a cousin to see you talk,
And no one feels an alarm, Tom,
    At a quiet cousinly walk.
But, Tom, you'll find out what I happen to know,
    That such walks often grow into straying,
And the voices of cousins are sometimes so low,
    Heaven only knows what they are saying.

How again there happens so often, Tom,
    Soft pressure of hands and of fingers,
And looks that are moulded to soften, Tom,
    And tones on which memory lingers.
So that before the walk is half over, the strings
    Of your heart are all called into play,
By the voice of those fair, divine, sisterly things
    In not quite the most brotherly way.

And the voice of a sister may bring to you, Tom,
    Such notes as the angels woo,
But I fear should your cousin sing to you, Tom,
    You'd take her for an angel too.
For so curious a note is this note of theirs,
    That you'd fancy the voice that gave it,
Was all the while singing the national airs,
    Instead of the Psalms of David.

I once had a cousin that sang to me, Tom,
    And her name shall be nameless now,
But the sound of that voice is still young, Tom,
    Though we are no longer so.
'Tis folly to dream of a lover of green
    When there's not a leaf on the tree,
But between singing and walking, that cousin has been—
    God forgive her—the ruin of me.

I'LL BE BEAUTIFUL.

'LL be beautiful!" she said,
    Softly a quaint old love-song singing,
Arching and nodding her pretty head,
O! she was so daintily bred!
    Golden curls to her fair brow clinging,
    Voice so bird-like, so clear and ringing!
        Lips so dewy and red.

"I'll be beautiful!" she sung;
    "Ruling my lovers with smiles and sighs,
They shall say that jewels drop from my tongue,
That of all the maidens I danced among
    None have such eloquent eyes;
    I care not to be either witty or wise—
        From such tears are rung."

"And I will be beautiful!" said May,
    Lifting her soft blue eyes to heaven;
"Dear Lord Jesus, Thou art the way!
I will be gentle in all I say,
    And pardon as I would be forgiven;
I'll strive to be purer, day by day,
        And in Thy strength—pray.

"I will be beautiful—in my heart,
    Roses and lilies are fair, but fading:
A chastened spirit is better than art
    To give young faces sweet tint and shading.
These for my beauty—a voice whose tone
    Shall be to the sad like a song;
An eye as ready to sparkle alone
    As when in the brilliant throng;
A smile as bright for the household few
    As the many in courtly hall;
For a smile if 'tis happy is always new;
    And a low voice pleaseth all.
What matter if tresses or eye grows dull!
If the heart be holy 'tis beautiful."

THE PETRIFIED FERN.

I N a valley, centuries ago,
Grew a little fern leaf, green and slender,
Veining delicate, and fibers tender—
    Waving when the wind crept down so low :
Bushes tall, and grass and moss grew round it ;
Playful sunbeams darted in and found it,
But no foot of man e'er came that way ;
Earth was young and keeping holiday.

    Useless? Lost? There came a thoughtful man
Searching nature's secrets far and deep.
From a fissure in a rocky steep
    He withdrew a stone on which there ran
Fairy pencilings, a quaint design—
Leafage, veining, flowers, clear and fine ;
And the fern's life lay in every line,
So, I think, God hides some lives away,
Sweetly to surprise us the last day.

IN ABSENCE.

ATCH her kindly, stars;
From the sweet protecting skies,
Follow her with tender eyes;
Look so lovingly that she
Cannot choose but think of me;
Watch her kindly, stars!

Soothe her sweetly, night;
On her eyes, o'erwearied, press
The tired lids, with light caress;
Let that shadowy hand of thine
Ever in her dreams seem mine;
Soothe her sweetly, night!

Wake her gently, morn;
Let the notes of early birds
Seem like Love's melodious words;
Every pleasant sound, my dear,
When she wakes from sleep, should hear;
Wake her gently, morn!

Kiss her softly, winds;
Softly, that she may not miss
Any sweet, accustomed bliss;
On her lips, her eyes, her face,
Till I come to take your place;
Kiss and kiss her, winds!

THE LITTLE PEOPLE.

A DREARY place would be this earth
    Were there no little people in it;
The song of life would lose its mirth,
    Were there no children to begin it.

No little forms like buds to grow,
    And make the admiring heart surrender;
No little hands on breast and brow,
    To keep the thrilling love-chords tender.

No babe within our arms to leap,
    No little feet toward slumber tending;
No little knee in prayer to bend,
    Our lips to theirs the sweet words lending.

What would the ladies do for work,
    Were there no pants or jackets tearing;
No tiny dresses to embroider:
    No cradle for their watchful caring?

No rosy boys at wintry-morn,
    With satchel to the school-house hasting;
No merry shouts as home they rush;
    No precious morsel for their tasting.

Tall, grave, grown people at the door,
    Tall, grave, grown people at the table;
The men on business all intent,
    The dames lugubrious as they're able.

The sterner souls would get more stern,
    Unfeeling natures more inhuman;
And men to stoic coldness turn,
    And woman would be less than woman.

Life's song indeed would lose its charm,
    Were there no babies to begin it;
A doleful place this world would be,
    Were there no little people in it.

NOT KNOWING.

KNOW not what will befall me! God hangs a mist
    o'er my eyes;
And o'er each step of my onward path he makes new
    scenes to rise;
And every joy he sends me comes as a sweet and glad
    surprise.

I see not a step before me as I tread in the days of
    the year;
But the Past is still in God's keeping; the Future
    his mercy shall clear;
And what looks dark in the distance may brighten
    as I draw near.

For perhaps the dreaded future has less bitterness than I think;
The Lord may sweeten the water before I stoop to drink;
Or, if Marah must be Marah, he will stand beside its brink.

It may be there is waiting for the coming of my feet,
Some gift of such rare blessedness, some joy so strangely sweet,
That my lips can only tremble with the thanks I cannot speak.

O restful, blissful Ignorance! 'Tis blessed not to know!
It keeps me quiet in those arms which will not let me go,
And hushes my soul to rest on the bosom which loves me so.

So I go on, not knowing! I would not if I might;
I would rather walk in the dark with God, than go alone in the light;
I would rather walk with him by faith than walk alone by sight.

My heart shrinks back from trials which the Future may disclose,
Yet, I never had a sorrow but what the dear Lord chose;
So I send the coming tears back with the whispered words, "He knows."

Leaves that are Fairest.

EAVES that are fairest
    Soonest decay,
Loved ones the rarest
    Soon pass away;
Smiles that are brightest
    Soonest grow cold,
Tales that are lightest
    Soonest are told.

But the leaf and the tale give us joy while they last,
And the smile of a friend makes a joy of the past;
For memory preserves in its tender embrace
The sunbeams of life as they flashed on his face.

Fortunes the proudest
    Fly with the years,
Laughter the loudest
    Softens to tears.

Joys the complctest
    Last but an hour,
Perfumes the sweetest
    Die with the flower.

But why should we sigh for the joys that have fled,
Or mourn the fond hopes that are lost with the dead?
Fresh hopes and new joys coming seasons will bring,
As perfumes will return with the roses of Spring.

G·O·O D - B Y.

OD be with you! through my losing
   And my grieving, shall I say?
Through my smiling and my hoping—
   God be with you, friends, to-day!

Somewhere, on a shore of silver,
   (God be with you on the way!)
In a sunlight sifted richly
   From a thousand skies of May.

In the meanings of the sunrise,
   In the soul of summer rain,
In the heart of purple hazes,
   We will not say Good-by again.

But the tears dash through my dreaming,
   And the thing I fain would say,
Falters into this—this only;
   God be with you till that day!

HOW STRANGE.

OW strange it will be, love, how strange when we
    two
  Shall be what all lovers become,
You frigid and faithless, I cold and untrue,
You thoughtless of me, and I careless of you,
Our pet names grown rusty with nothing to do,
Love's bright web unravelled, and rent, and worn
    through,
  And life's loom left empty—ah, hum!
    Ah, me,
  How strange it will be!

How strange it will be when the witchery goes,
  Which makes me seem lovely to-day;
When your thought of me loses its COULEUR DE ROSÉ,
When every day serves some new fault to disclose,
When you find I've cold eyes and an every day nose,
And wonder you could for a moment suppose
  I was out of the commonplace way;
    Ah, me,
  How strange it will be.

How strange it will be love—how strange when we meet,
   With just a chill touch of the hand !
When my pulses no longer delightedly beat
At the thought of your coming, the sound of your feet,
When I watch not your going, far down the long street,
When your dear, loving voice, now so thrillingly sweet,
   Grows harsh in reproach or command ;
      Ah, me,
    How strange it will be !

How strange it will be when we willingly stay
   Divided the weary day through !
Or, getting remotely apart as we may,
Sit chilly and silent, with nothing to say,
Or cooly converse on the news of the day
In a wearisome, old married folks sort of way!
   I shrink from the picture ; don't you ?
      Ah, me,
    How strange it will be !

Dear love, if our hearts DO grow torpid and old,
   As so many others have done ;
If we let our love perish with hunger and cold,
If we dim all life's diamonds and tarnish its gold,
If we choose to live wretched and die unconsoled
'Twill be strangest of all things that ever were told
   As happening under the sun !
      Ah, me,
    How strange it WILL be !

One of the Sweet Old Chapters.

ONE of the sweet old chapters,
    After a day like this;
The day brought tears and trouble,
    The evening brings no kiss.

No rest in the arms I long for—
    Rest and refuge and home;
Grieved, and lonely, and weary,
    Unto the Book I come.

One of the sweet old chapters,
    The love that blossoms through
His care of the birds and lilies,
    Out in the meadow dew.

His evening lies soft around them;
    Their faith is simply to be.
O, hushed by the tender lesson,
    My God, let me rest in thee!

www.ingramcontent.com/pod-product-compliance
Lightning Source LLC
Chambersburg PA
CBHW021558270326
41931CB00009B/1275

* 9 7 8 3 3 3 7 2 6 5 5 4 0 *